LEARN FOOTBALL
WITH JACK CHARLTON

LEARN FOOTBALL
WITH JACK CHARLTON

Stanley Paul
London Sydney Auckland Johannesburg

Photograph Acknowledgements

Thanks are due to the following for allowing the use of copyright photographs: AllSport (John Barnes), Mark Leech (Peter Shilton), Duncan Raban (Nigel Clough), Sporting Pictures (UK) Ltd (Glenn Hoddle, Frank Stapleton, Kevin Sheedy, Ruud Gullit), Bob Thomas (Marco Van Basten). The specially taken photographs are by courtesy of Tyne Tees Television

Stanley Paul and Co. Ltd

An imprint of Century Hutchinson

Brookmount House, 62-65 Chandos Place,
Covent Garden, London WC2N 4NW

Century Hutchinson Australia (Pty) Ltd
88-91 Albion Street, Surry Hills, NSW 2010

Century Hutchinson New Zealand Limited
191 Archers Road, PO Box 40-086, Glenfield, Auckland 10

Century Hutchinson South Africa (Pty) Ltd
PO Box 337, Bergvlei 2012, South Africa

First published 1978
Reprinted 1979 (twice), 1980
Revised edition 1989
Copyright © Tyne Tees Television Ltd
(a member of the Trident Group) 1978, 1989

Phototypeset in Century Schoolbook by
Input Typesetting Ltd, London SW19 8DR

Printed and bound in Great Britain by
Scotprint Ltd, Musselburgh

British Library Cataloguing in Publication Data

Charlton, Jack
  Learn association football with Jack
  Charlton. – Rev. ed.
  1. Association football – Manuals
  I. Title
  796.334′2

  ISBN 0 09 174027 4

This book was originally based on the
Tyne Tees Television series
Play Soccer Jack Charlton's Way

Contents

Introduction

When managing the Republic of Ireland team during the European Championships in West Germany I was reminded that it is impossible to succeed in football without a mastery of the basic techniques.

I played thirty-six times for my country and helped England to win the World Cup. I have won Cup Winners' medals and League Championships, and have been successful in European competitions. I played professionally for twenty-five years, yet I was still trying to improve the day before I retired.

When Don Revie managed Leeds United he would always take us back to basics during pre-season training. And that at a time when he could call on fifteen international players. Without good technique football cannot be enjoyed. The more we practise the better we get.

In this book I have attempted to outline the basics. Learn to apply them and your game will improve. The younger the better. There will never be a perfect player. No one will ever completely master the game. But by achieving a higher standard of individual skill you will enhance the prospects of your team.

I hope you enjoy the book.

Jack Charlton

1 Using space and equipment

Portable equipment is invaluable when learning how to organize and instruct young footballers.

The simplest and cheapest equipment is often the best, but you must make the best use of it.

It doesn't matter whether you are dealing with schoolboys, youths or simply lads who love the game. You can improve their skills with simple equipment that will help you to stimulate interest and vary routines.

Bollards are very useful – the rubber, polythene or synthetic ones used to mark roads and closed-off areas. It isn't always practical to draw lines. With a dozen or so bollards you can mark out a pitch, altering its shape and size in a matter of seconds.

Poles of varying heights can be used as goal-posts or corner flags. By slotting a pole through the top of a bollard you have a portable goal-post. You can also play three or four mini-games by quartering off your playing area.

This enables you to stage games of six or seven a side in realistic circumstances. You can control this number of men easily. Use bollards and poles to mark out an area in which games can be played and where practices can be held.

If you are familiar with the grid system of coaching – the use of squares with activity going on inside – you will know the practical benefit in using these for setting up practices for shooting, dribbling and ball control.

Bollards are designed not to blow over in the wind, and should anyone fall on them there is no threat of injury. Two large poles can be driven into the ground through the centre of them to make perfect goals of the appropriate size. For instance, I hate to see

eight- or nine-year-old goalkeepers in a full-size goal.

To encourage very young children to practise, the simple wall is ideal. Every technique can be practised individually by varying the service, either throwing or

If space is restricted you can organize four mini-games by quartering off your playing area

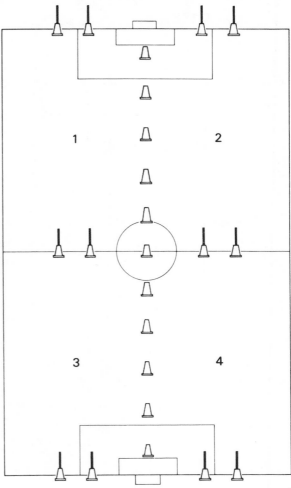

▲ *The use of two large
poles provides young
players with a more
reasonable size of goal.
Here we see that the
forward is forced to
sharpen his finishing to
find room between the
advancing goalkeeper
and the two posts*

▶ *Two boys, a ball and a
wall – there is no limit
to the variety of shots,
passes and chips the boys
can produce for each
other*

The use of portable equipment such as bollards ▲
is invaluable when organizing a large group of
young players – also as many footballs as
possible

The wall can also be used for heading work. ◄
Either count how many times you can head the
ball against the wall without a break; or head
the ball to each other, using the wall to glance
the ball back and forth as if it were a third player

kicking a ball against the wall. A couple of
kids left to use their imagination can get a
lot out of this.

Most schools and sports clubs have tennis
courts which are not in use during the winter
months. These *can* be used to put on football
practices. The kids won't have the problem
of chasing footballs over large areas. They
are usually of a size that not only encourages
passing movements but also allows long
kicks and high kicks which will always help
with the control.

If the money is available, floodlights, one
either end, will greatly increase the scope
when using these courts.

It is a good idea to look around your school.
There may be an area that is not often used
because it is not the correct size. By using

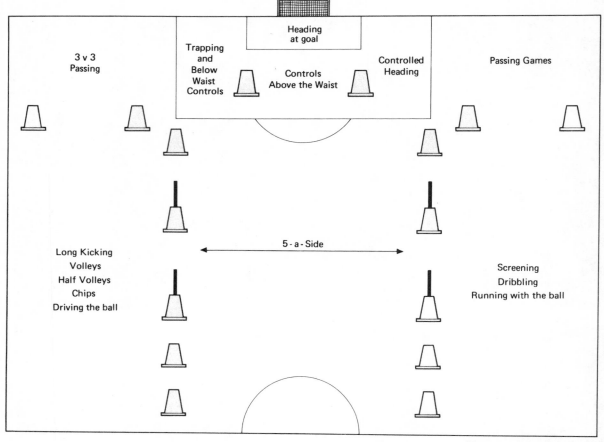

3 v 3
Passing

Trapping
and
Below
Waist
Controls

Heading
at goal

Controls
Above the Waist

Controlled
Heading

Passing Games

Long Kicking
Volleys
Half Volleys
Chips
Driving the ball

5 - a - Side

Screening
Dribbling
Running with the ball

Allow ten minutes in each area.

some of the equipment I have mentioned, you may find you have good facilities.

It is important when teaching technique and skills to have as many footballs as possible. One ball amongst twenty-two will not give the kids many kicks or chances to improve their control. A dozen balls between the same number will ensure they have many more opportunities.

And I really mean footballs, not the light plastic floaty kind. These are virtually useless. The ball we practise with should be as near as possible to the ball used in a game. In all the techniques you will find that a sense of touch and feel is essential. You can't get this when practising with the light plastic balls.

Once you have the equipment, study the area in which you are going to work. The next essential is encouragement.

Kids learn quickly: given the opportunity, they will improve. If space is restricted use the area as it is marked in the two diagrams.

Although we have shown how skills can be practised in the squares, you aren't restricted. This system helps to keep the kids interested. Having worked in one square at one particular skill they progress to another and at some stage they will play a game.

Kids will play football for ever, but they should be given a change of programme. This system works beautifully, simplifying the job of the coach or teacher.

2 Passing

A pass can travel anything between six feet and sixty yards, further if you like. But when we talk about passing we really mean short passes, passes that travel no more than twenty to twenty-five yards and are hit with the inside or the outside of the foot – even a back heel or a toe prod.

Passing cannot be divorced from control. Most passes are made when the ball is actually moving or while it is being brought under control. It is a bit like the chicken and the egg. Which comes first, the pass or the control?

In order to pass you first need to have the ball under control. In order to control the ball you have to receive it from someone. I always encourage players to pass with their good foot. If you are right-footed don't try to make passes with the left if it is possible to make them with the right. Your balance foot is usually your left if you are a right-footed player.

It is possible to pass through an area of 360 degrees without actually standing off your left foot, which again is your balance foot. By using the inside of the foot, we can go from almost behind us from the left-hand side to almost 45 degrees in front of us. From there we can go to the right without moving the left foot at all, playing the ball with the outside of the right foot. To complete a full 360 degrees, back heel the ball.

Passing with the inside of the foot provides the passer with a tremendous range or area. This pass will finish up wide to the passer's left

Here the inside-foot pass is going forward

▲ *Now a switch to the use of the outside of the foot, switching the direction of the pass to the opposite side, the passer's right*

▶ *A little bit of cheeky skill here, using the back-heel pass to find a team-mate positioned behind you. But make sure you know where your team-mate is standing*

Vision is controlling the ball, looking around and deciding exactly what pass is needed. Here the player with the ball pushes a side-foot pass back to his goalkeeper from the eighteen-yard line

This pass is more firmly struck, but the player is still in control of the ball and knows what weight he has put behind his pass

There are a number of critical factors in passing. There is 'weighting' of the ball, or how fast the ball must travel if the pass is to be a good one. When passing to a person standing still the ball needs to be played quickly but not so quickly that it will be difficult to control. A player who is moving, say a winger going down the touchline, will probably need the ball five or ten yards in front of him. It is important that the pass coincides with the run that is being made.

The back heel is a blind pass. So we must know exactly where it is going. With this one we tend to feel for the ball a little bit, just a little nudge with the back heel for someone coming from behind.

When passing back to the goalkeeper from the edge of the eighteen-yard box, the ball should be played a little more firmly.

Remember the word *vision*. Vision is controlling the ball, and having a look around before deciding what to do: a pass with the inside of the foot, a pass with the outside, a back heel, a long kick, a chip. Whatever we decide, it is most important to look first.

It isn't necessary to place the left foot right next to the ball as long as the ball is within easy playing distance. We only need to adjust the balance. We adjust the balance

Opponents usually attempt to prevent you making a pass. Do not allow an opponent to get too close before you play the ball. Be aware of those players around you, friend and foe

Note how the player about to receive this pass on his left foot keeps his eyes on the ball and steadies his balance on his right foot. This is important

through movement. There are few opportunities to control when standing still. So having controlled the ball we should have movement. This is the time when we are adjusting our balance, looking around and deciding what to do next.

What makes a good pass? Well, first of all accuracy. The pass must be accurate, it must be correctly weighted so that we can improve the situation or create one that someone else can exploit.

We are normally confronted by an opponent. We mustn't let him come close enough to obstruct the pass. We need to pass the ball when the player coming towards us is no more than a yard or two away.

If you can imagine an opponent standing and putting out his left foot then our angle of pass must be such that his foot doesn't impede the path of the ball. Don't let him get too close before making the pass.

This brings us to the use of angles. Good ball control helps in this, because if an opponent starts to come across the line we use control to take the ball wider, preventing him from making an interception.

Players should help each other by opening up angles. Nigel Clough, son of the Nottingham Forest manager, Brian Clough,

Sometimes it is necessary to dribble the ball wide of a challenging opponent before making a pass. Here the challenger is cutting down the passer's angle, so the passer goes wide of him, then passes to a team-mate who has found a little room

Here the player on the ball is looking for the best passing opening. He needs his team-mates' co-operation, because unless they provide him with good angles he may attempt a risky pass and give the ball away

and already an England Under–21 international, does this naturally. He has a highly developed positional sense and is invariably where he can be seen by the other Forest players.

Practices

How do we learn the technique of passing? It is best practised in small-sided team games. If children are not very good at passing, then give them an area of maybe fifteen yards square and allow them to play a three against one. This gives them plenty of time to control the ball and have a look around before they are actually put under real pressure.

As they improve their passing techniques – learning not to let players get too close to

◄ Nigel Clough *(Nottingham Forest and England Under-21) showing the positional sense that makes him easy to find with a pass*

The player on the ball is confronted by an opponent who blocks his way. A team-mate, seeing the situation arising, moves wide so that he is available to receive a pass. Now the challenging opponent cannot intercept

It is not always possible to go forward. Here the man on the ball is blocked. So he must turn out of trouble and lay the ball back to his team-mate, who can be seen moving away from his marker to take up a good position behind the man on the ball. This is good support play

them – their control and their vision, we can increase the pressure. Three against two, going on to three against three.

Kids get bored with passing games that have no object. Give them a target. Do this by putting up a little goal, using one of them as a goalkeeper. They can then play three against one with a target to aim at. It means that they have now got to work hard at making angles when supporting each other from behind and when making forward runs. It helps to extend the range of passing movements and develops the qualities essential to good passing.

Practice makes perfect, and we can't do too much of the right kind. We must insist on quality. The passes, the movement and the ball control must be good. Emphasize vision. Know where everyone is as you receive the ball, know where they are when you have got the ball. Weight your passes correctly, learn when to deliver, how to deliver. Push for quality all the time.

Small-sided team games are a great help – anything from two against two to seven against seven. When we get into larger areas we encourage a different type of pass, a longer kick. Practise short passing in small areas but an area that suits the size of the kids and their degree of skill. Certainly no less than ten yards by ten yards.

Passing movements include such things as wall passes, through passes and setting-up passes, but these are outside the scope of this book. We are mostly concerned with quality of passing.

The use of support in passing movements

One further point about small-sided team games: the player on the ball must be supported. It isn't always possible to play the ball forward. You can turn out of a tight situation and lay the ball back to someone who is supporting. He may then be able to deliver a pass elsewhere.

Stick to the things that we have talked about and remember the words **vision, control, balance**. If you are right-footed use your right foot whenever possible. Play to your strengths and use them well.

This sequence of pictures shows the value of good support, sharp vision and intelligent teamwork. Seeing his avenues closed, the player on the ball turns back, loses his marker for a few seconds and lays a good, firm pass with the inside of his left foot to a team-mate in support. The angle is good because the player who receives the pass has time to control the ball, aim and shoot before the defender can get across. This time the goalkeeper saves

3 Control

Good control gains time, time to look around, to take evading action. Time in which to select the most effective pass. Glenn Hoddle, the Monaco and England midfield player, has time because he has achieved absolute mastery over the ball. No matter how the ball arrives, Hoddle has it instantly under control.

◀ Glenn Hoddle *(Monaco and England) displays the sensitive touch that gives mastery of the ball*

▼ *Underfoot control is shown in these three pictures. Note the balance and eyes on the ball with the foot raised in preparation for taking the pace off the ball. Once the ball has been 'killed' by the sole of the boot the movement follows through as the player moves into a position of control, placing the foot on the ball to keep possession*

Most players when controlling the ball tend to stand and wait. They should be encouraged to go forward and control as quickly as possible. The sooner you get to the ball the better. When we talk about controlling the ball below the waist we mean with the feet, the shins and the thighs, with the outside and inside of the foot, keeping your balance. It is almost impossible to control the ball well if we aren't prepared, knowing exactly which method we are going to use. Be aware, be on the move – alive to the ball as it comes. Develop a soft touch and learn to take the pace off the ball.

Underfoot control is where we let the ball bounce, holding our foot just over the bounce. Let the ball hit the underside of the foot and leave it where it is.

We can control the ball 45 degrees to the left or right, but keep it simple and soft.

Control with the side of the foot is based on the same simple principle of taking the steam out of the ball. As the ball approaches, allow it to bounce, then guide the outside of the boot against the ball and turn it away into the path you wish to take. Remember that control does not mean using your leg like a brick wall. Relax the muscles and soften the ball's contact. Otherwise it will bounce away as quickly as it arrived

Here we see the same process in action. But this time the player wants to take the ball to his left. Again keep your eyes on the ball, make sure you are properly balanced and comfortable, then move into the ball's flight and bring it under control, turning it as it bounces

In order to take the ball away from a challenge coming in from the left, use the side of the foot instead of the sole of the foot.

The ball is coming straight at us and we want to take it to the right. As the ball bounces, control it away at an angle with the outside of the right foot. If we want to take it to the left then the same applies. As the ball bounces use the inside of the foot to take it away to the left, as you see in the photographs.

Using this technique we can almost go a full circle. To complete the 360 degrees nudge the ball back in the direction we want

to go. Always try to get the body in line with the ball.

If the first attempt at controlling the ball is clumsy, at least we have a chance to recover. The bouncing ball may hit the body, but at least it stays with us.

We have to control balls that are pitching to the right or left of us. Let the ball bounce, reach for it with the inside of the foot by stretching out the leg. Controlling with the inside of the left foot is a simple one and can be done with your bad foot. It's easier than trying to use the outside of your right foot because then it is impossible to balance properly.

The 'good foot' is the foot we use for kicking. If you are a right-footed player the left foot will be the balance foot, and you must be well-balanced. The converse applies to left-footed players.

On a wet ground it is as well to let the ball hit us on the shin, just flexing the knees so that we keep the ball down. Let the ball hit the body.

Learn to control the ball with the thigh. It is important that we can control the ball when facing where we want to go.

If a ball is coming out of the air, control it with the thigh so that it drops in front of you. Put a little bit of impulsion to the ball. Nudge it in the right direction straight away.

If we want to go to the right, let the ball hit the thigh and as it does so bring the leg away, giving slightly to get that soft control. At the same time bend or lean so that the ball comes off in the right direction.

For example, if we want to take it to the right we put the thigh at the ball, but turning it so that the ball drops to our right-hand side. To go to the left the same thing applies: knee up to the ball, take away as the ball hits the thigh and roll it off to the left. Look at the photographs on page 23.

In all ball control we need movement. We must be controlling and turning away from the opposition. Turn and control in one movement. Occasionally we use the thigh for

Using the inside and outside of the foot, nudge the ball into the path you wish to take. Get in line with the flight of the ball and your control will be made that much easier

By keeping the body in line with the ball, you get a better chance of controlling the ball if you need a second attempt. If the ball bounces badly, for example, you can use your controlling foot quickly to bring the ball down

Sometimes it is better to allow the ball to hit you on the shin or just below the knee. This way you keep the ball down and make control much easier. Again remember to cushion the ball rather than block its flight

knocking the ball upwards so that it can be volleyed clear or headed to someone.

Another way to control the ball, although we see little of it in Britain, is with the instep. Put the instep at the ball and, just as it makes contact, take the foot away so that the ball is cushioned. This is a very difficult technique to master, but once mastered it is probably one of the best-looking skills, one that all the best players are equipped with.

Remember all we have said about ball control – selecting how we intend to deal with the ball is important, being gentle with the ball, taking the pace from it.

But most of all, select a control to suit the situation.

If the ball comes at you at a height which makes leg control impossible, use your body. The chest is a strong and wide area on which to cushion a ball. Use your body to direct the ball downwards. Again control is made so much easier

Here we see the technique used both to control the ball on the thigh and to guide it to the right or left at the same time. Just the slightest nudge can do the trick. Also move into the ball as it drops, so that after the first contact you can determine the direction in which the ball will go either by moving the leg away quickly or by moving the leg slightly left or right

Practices

1 Using a wall, volley or kick the ball, always going to meet it.
2 Throw a ball in the air, chase it, control it. Bring the ball back or take the ball away to the side using the techniques we have talked about earlier in this chapter.

3 If you have two, three or four players, get them to serve the ball for each other, introducing opposition so that the player is aware of challenge. (Only introduce opposition when technique is up to standard. It is no good introducing opposition if the player hasn't perfected the skills of trapping and turning with the ball. So it is very important that techniques are

practised, understood and applied before we get ambitious.)

It is a good idea to condition games. Insist that goalkeepers, instead of rolling the ball out, kick or throw it in the air. This will encourage various types of ball control.

One thing is certain. You will only improve technique and timing by working at skills over and over and over again. Move to the ball, control it, and by making mistakes learn not to make mistakes. Practise, practise and practise, until good ball control becomes an automatic part of your game.

The thigh can be used to move the ball into a suitable position for a volley. You can flick the ball up or sideways with your thigh, then shoot for goal. Again it is important to turn as you control the ball, so eliminating the problems of having to do this from a static position

If the ball drops too far ahead for using the thigh, use the instep to cushion the fall then take the foot away, leaving the ball in front and nicely set up for a shot or pass. This type of control can also vary so that as you cushion the ball's fall you guide it down with your foot in a swift, easy movement

4 Heading

Confidence when applied to heading is *very* important. If kids are badly taught they will finish up misheading. Balls that are headed badly tend to hurt. This drains confidence. We should be aiming to develop techniques that will allow players to head a ball comfortably and without pain.

Apply these four points: 1. Keep your eyes open. 2. Have good balance so that you get in line with the ball and head with the forehead, almost right between the eyes. 3. Keep the neck, back and trunk in a very solid straight line. Don't wave about. 4. Heading must be very positive.

Start by not serving the ball too hard, build up confidence and show kids that there is nothing to fear when heading. You'll find that they improve dramatically.

Never encourage kids to jump to head if they can do it when their feet are on the

Eyes on the ball, body properly balanced and a positive action of going to head the ball rather than waiting for the ball to hit your forehead

ground. This keeps their balance and positioning.

The ball between the eyes is important. I get the kids to wet a small patch between the eyes and then get them to wave their hand in front of it. The patch goes cold and they know exactly where the ball should be headed.

Know where you want to head the ball before it gets to you. In other words, look before you head. Good movement and balance will always help, but it's also important to know where you intend the ball to go.

Most heading is positive – we only get one touch at the ball. Remember, your eyes close automatically on impact.

Good movement and balance are vital. Move like a boxer, putting yourself in position, not allowing the head to wave about but keeping it nice and solid. Frank Stapleton, who did such an excellent job for the Republic of Ireland in the 1988 European Championships, perfected his headwork

Do not jump to head a ball if you can head it while your feet are on the ground. You achieve a better balance when your feet are on the ground. And always try to see where you are going to head the ball rather than just attempting to thump it straight back

Deflection heading is important. Here you turn your body with the ball. As it comes, get in line, head it as instructed but also turn your body into the direction you wish to send the ball. Now you are guiding the ball's flight with your whole body

A good example of control heading: seeing where your team-mates are and deliberately heading the ball to them, either by turning your body to direct the ball firmly or by glancing the ball off your forehead with a flick of the head

when playing for Arsenal and it has served him well. Sometimes it is necessary to deflect the ball, which Frank does brilliantly, but this is still done with the forehead. Try to play the ball in the direction that you can see by following the ball around.

Controlled headers are those where we look around as the ball is coming, see a player and knock the ball to him. This is known as control heading.

Deflection heading is similar. Think of a centre-half dealing with a ball that is crossed across the face of his goal. He does not want to head it straight back but to deflect it across and away. He still hits the ball in exactly the same way, but not with only the head moving. It is done by turning the body to follow the line of the ball. Watch it come, move the body into line – then head.

Frank Stapleton (*Le Havre and Republic of Ireland*). *Heads up – but Stapleton gets there first – the goal threatened*

Heading down can be a little more complicated. ▲
Get above the ball and direct it downwards. But do not rush this, otherwise you may hurt your nose. Always keep those eyes on the ball; do not allow the ball to bounce off you

Distance heading involves watching the ball very ◄
carefully and using both legs and back to increase power. Punch that ball away with the area of forehead between the eyes. Strength and balance are important here. Otherwise the ball may shoot up in the air or deflect away to an opponent. Be positive

When heading for distance, watch the ball carefully. It is important that we head the ball as far away from our goal as possible. This is achieved by using the power of the legs and the back to push at the ball between the eyes, with the forehead.

Heading for goal involves confidence, accuracy ▼
and single-mindedness. Go for the ball, don't wait for it. Get up properly and keep the ball between your eyes. Aim for the part of the goal you want to hit. Do not allow your eyes to wander on to the goalkeeper. Let him worry about your header. Head the ball properly and it will never hurt you. You are the boss

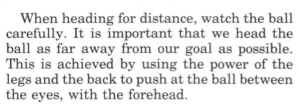

5 Goalkeeping

Goalkeeping is a very specialized job. We tend to say in the game that goalkeepers have to be a little bit mad. In many cases this is true. Certainly they have got to be really dedicated.

Essentials for a goalkeeper are a good pair of hands, courage, an appreciation of angles, alertness, anticipation and sharp reactions. But most of all they must like work.

Peter Shilton of Derby County and England was fortunate to understudy Gordon Banks, the greatest goalkeeper of my time, when they were together at Leicester City. Peter was a quick learner but he could not have achieved so much in the game without hours and hours on the practice ground and in the gymnasium, sharpening his reflexes and building his strength.

There aren't many techniques to learn, only those of kicking out of the hands, kicking balls that are on the ground, and getting in line with the ball. Mainly it is practice, learning how to catch crosses, how to narrow angles, how to anticipate shots.

Goalkeepers should always catch a ball if possible, and then immediately pull it into the chest, so that if they are challenged, pushed or bumped they are less likely to fumble.

If the ball is just a little bit too far out to catch, punch it. Punching is reaching out with one hand or two, to propel the ball as far away as possible from the goal. Punching is usually used only when the goalkeeper is under pressure and might not be able to catch the ball cleanly.

Goalkeepers must learn to throw the ball correctly. The players receiving the ball should be facing the way they want to go, so

Here we see two methods of gathering the ball to your chest. The first shows the goalkeeper going down on one knee and getting his body behind the ball; the second shows him down on both knees and leaning forward to meet the ball. Always get your body in line with the shot and keep your legs together as much as possible without losing balance

With the high ball, use both hands, keep both eyes on the ball, not the on-rushing forward, and immediately pull that ball down to your chest. Now it is under your absolute control. Do not be careless with that ball. Make it yours first, then distribute as you wish

Peter Shilton (*Derby County and England*). Agility and sharp reflexes developed by hard work helped Shilton become an outstanding goalkeeper

Coming out for a ball under pressure is always difficult. But make up your mind what you are going to do and stick by that decision. If you decide to punch the ball, keep your eyes on it and go for power as well as accuracy. Get the ball out of your area. Naturally the catch is always better, but if attempting to catch the ball involves the risk of dropping it, then by all means punch

Goalkeepers must learn to make angles in the same way outfield players do. By advancing off your line you cut down the angles open to the forward; by taking up a position on your near post you dictate to the forward where he can and cannot put the ball; good goalkeepers even stand more to one side of their goal and invite the forward to shoot for the other side. By deliberately moving across in one direction the goalkeeper is ready for the shot aimed for the area he has vacated

If you stay on your line all the time, shots at goal can still be saved, but if you get a hand to the ball without catching it the chances are it will roll into the net. But if you come off your line and cut down the forward's angle, a touch to his shot has more chance of deflecting wide of the goal and outside a post

make sure that the ball travels to them as in a pass, quickly and accurately.

Goalkeepers must know about angles. The photographs opposite show you how to go about it.

If we stand on the line to make a save and the ball is hit past us at an angle, it will go into the goal. By moving three or four yards towards the ball there is a good chance that we can touch it wide of the post. This is what is called narrowing the angle.

Sometimes for a hanging ball we need to jump to make a catch, or put our fingertips to the ball, turning it over the cross bar as we would when playing volleyball. Use your hands to help the ball on.

A goalkeeper is a director. He directs the play in front of him, he tells his full-backs where he wants them on the line, he tells his centre-half who should be marked, he makes sure that people aren't left unmarked.

A good call will also help to get defenders out of trouble. Then they can run, turn, clear the ball or play it back to the goalkeeper. Yes, he can be a director helping everyone around him because he is facing the play. You can't put too much emphasis on the amount of practice a goalkeeper should get. He should be encouraged to work with everyone, especially on shooting practices. The goalkeeper should always be allowed to work at his game.

6 Kicking

This chapter is about kicking. We must learn to drive the ball when shooting or sending it quickly to our left or right.

The technique is simple. There are principles to be applied. If the knee is over the ball it will keep low. How we approach the ball is important. It is difficult to drive the ball when coming straight at it. It's much better to approach the ball at an angle, left or right, depending on which foot you are kicking with.

Put the knee over the ball, try to get the head over the ball, then kick through. If this is done correctly the ball will travel low and we can control the power.

▼ *The driving kick needs to be kept low, certainly below cross-bar level. So keep your knee over the ball as you kick it. Point the big toe on your shooting foot, get your head over the ball and approach the ball from a comfortable angle, depending on whether you are right- or left-footed. Now your shot will be low and straight*

Keeping the head over the ball helps to keep the ▲ *ball low. But if you want to make a distance kick, say, to make a clearance from your own area, keep your head back. The ball will travel onwards. Again, line up your foot with the ball and strike the ball cleanly. The principles of kicking do not change*

The position of the head is very important. We need to be over the top of the ball. When trying to get the ball into the air the head must be back, away from the ball. Lean back so that the ball is kicked on the up. Place the standing foot where you feel most comfortable. Concentrate on a good follow-through and, as your head goes back, the ball will rise. Approach from an angle, and allow the natural swing of the foot to send the ball in the right direction.

It isn't necessary to keep your eyes on the ball. Once you start the approach your mind is like a computer. It takes everything into consideration – where your foot has to go down and how hard you need to kick. It passes the information on and the action

Here we see the kick-through. The foot follows the flight of the ball. The head is held back and the body is well balanced

becomes automatic. The selection is processed and produced.

A follow-through is essential to long kicking. This gives direction and extra power.

The Chip

Now the chip. This gets the ball into the air quickly. It's like using an axe. We chop down behind the ball, making contact as we come down so that back spin is applied. The ball rises quickly. When it bounces instead of rolling on, as it would when top spin is applied, the ball stops sharply.

This is the sort of pass we might play over a defender for a winger to run on to when there isn't much room between the full-back and the dead-ball line.

Back spin stops the ball quickly, allowing the player to catch it before it runs out of play. We don't follow through. It's a chopping action. The strength you apply determines how far the ball will go.

There is another type of chip. Standing still on the ball, perhaps after controlling it, and with the ball directly in front of us we are ready to move off. Instead we decide to chip. This is done by putting the toe end under the ball and stabbing it, kicking down and under. This is not much use for distance. We use it to get a ball up quickly, over short distances, maybe fifteen or twenty yards.

A chip is one of the most rewarding passes. It can be extremely accurate.

Volleys

There are several types of volley.

A *half volley* is when we strike the ball at the instant it hits the ground. It is a difficult kick to control, to keep down. The timing must be perfect. I tend to discourage the half volley when shooting at goal because unless

35

The chip involves bringing the kicking foot down behind the ball like an axe. The foot chops down behind the ball, applying back spin. The ball will rise quickly and will not roll on loosely when it drops back on to the pitch. The back spin acts as a brake and the ball drops well within the area you aimed for

The short-distance chip is slightly different. Here you place your toe behind the ball and stab it upwards. This does not achieve any great distance, but as a chip to play from a standing position it can be both effective and very accurate

the ball is perfectly hit it will invariably rise over the bar.

I prefer *full volleys*. This is when the ball is struck in mid-air. Marco Van Basten, the AC Milan forward, demonstrated this skill most vividly when scoring a marvellous goal for Holland against the Soviet Union in the

Marco Van Basten *(AC Milan and Holland). The perfect striker. Balance, poise and power. A volley on its way*

Final of the European Championships. From what appeared to be an impossible angle he struck the ball on the 'full' and sent it into the top far corner. Luck? Possibly. But he had the confidence to go for the shot and he was rewarded with the most spectacular goal of the competition.

The volley is a tremendous shot. The ball is off the ground when struck and as long as you get head and knee over the ball it will travel low and straight. The volley is a stabbing motion. You do not actually follow through, especially if you want to keep the ball low

By throwing the knee and head over the ball, a volley can be kept low. We are able to strike the whole of the ball. The volley is a stabbing action with very little follow-through.

In *volleying for distance* the same principle applies. If the head is over the ball and the knee, it will keep low. If we lean back from the ball, kick through and follow through, the ball will rise. We use this one for long clearances. Lean back, follow through and turn on the power.

Volleying when the ball bounces. It's difficult to volley balls that are rising. To do this we launch ourselves at the ball, throwing our knee and head over, fighting to keep the ball down. This is a difficult volley to learn.

The same principles apply when volleying to the side, left or right – keep the ball low, put the foot where it feels most comfortable, watch the ball carefully and get your knee as far over the ball as possible.

The same applies when clearing with a volley as for volley shooting or passing from

Volleying for distance is another matter. If you are trying to get the ball far away from your area, lean back and strike the ball cleanly. This time do follow through. The ball will travel as far as the power you have put behind your shot

Volleying to the side, either left or right, is best done with the knee as much as possible over the ball. It is not possible to get your head over the ball as well because you will be automatically leaning away from the ball to help your balance. But the properly positioned knee is good enough

The volley struck as the ball bounces up off the pitch requires swift action. Get your body over the ball quickly

Clearing the ball from the side involves a different technique. You will be leaning away from the ball again, but this time kick up and follow through. This will lift the ball into the air and safely clear a defensive position

the side. We are automatically leaning away from the ball when it is in position. Instead of getting the knee over the ball, we kick up and follow through. This will get the ball into the air over a long distance.

Swerves

The Brazilians are famous for being able to 'bend' the ball. Some players do this better

The exciting Brazilian-style swerve can be applied by striking the ball off centre, either left to right as shown by the picture where the ball is being struck with the outside of the right foot, or right to left where the ball is struck with the inside of the right foot. When you have struck the ball, allow your foot to continue through its journey. This applies the spin necessary to move the ball as you wish. Obviously it does not matter which foot you use – the process is the same

40

than others. Kevin Sheedy, the Everton and Republic of Ireland midfield player, does it better than most and has scored some spectacular free kicks.

Kevin Sheedy *(Everton and Republic of Ireland). An educated left foot, Sheedy sends in a tormenting free kick*

The Brazilians practise this a lot and are therefore experts. It means striking the ball slightly off centre. Using the right foot, strike off centre to the right-hand side and let the foot continue through. The ball will spin and it is the spin that actually produces the swerve.

To swerve the ball from left to right, we strike it slightly off centre with the outside of the right foot and spin the ball the other

41

Bending the ball when passing is effective and accurate. With the correct strike and swerve the ball will move to the right or left of a defender and curl back to a central path by the time it gets behind him

Remember the importance of correctly weighting your pass: no matter how accurate it may be, if the player you are passing to cannot control the ball the exercise is pointless. Always think of the man you are passing to . Do not overdo the power behind the pass. Approach the ball slightly from the side and you will ensure that it straightens out by the time it reaches your teammate

way. Not a complicated kick, but an effective one.

It helps to open up angles when passing. If the angle is narrow, bend the ball a little bit more to the right.

Two things to remember when kicking. The weighting of the kick is important. This ensures that the ball travels at a speed that makes it easy to control. Remember the angle of approach to the ball, slightly from the side. This will straighten the ball out and send it in the right direction.

7 Control above the waist

None of the players who appeared in the 1988 European Championships made a greater impression than Ruud Gullit, the Dutchman who plays for AC Milan. He is a tremendous athlete and the best player with his chest I have seen since Pele. Gullit can control the ball like this even when travelling at top speed, often leaping to receive it in mid-air.

We can achieve a similar if less spectacular result by letting the ball bounce and hit the chest. By turning the body to right or left, the ball drops off at an angle. Chest control means exactly that. Keep the arms

Control above the waist is important – not only to trap the ball on your chest but also to be able to guide the ball off your chest into the direction you wish to go

This is done by turning your body as the ball is cushioned on your chest. This directs the ball to the right or left . . . or indeed straight ahead if that's where you want to go. But remember that a chest trap means what it says. Keep those arms wide and well away from the ball. This also aids balance

Chest control is more varied than many people imagine. You can pass the ball off your chest by deflecting it back to a team-mate. You can chest it down to your own feet, direct it upwards and volley the ball or even glance the ball up off your chest, duck under it and turn. This enables you to change direction

Ruud Gullit (AC Milan and Holland). Eyes on the ball, Gullit prepares to receive a lofted pass on his chest ▶

Control with the head is a little difficult at first, but can be achieved. Allow your knees to bend as the ball drops down on your head. This takes the

weight off the ball and when it drops you can achieve quick control with either foot

When the ball comes at you rather than down on you, use your head as the cushion. It's like heading in reverse. Instead of going at the ball, lean back slightly and allow the ball to drop off

your forehead. But do keep your eyes on the ball as it arrives. Relax your body as the ball comes. Again this takes the weight off the ball and it will drop rather than rebound

Head tennis or working with a pal who throws the ball at different heights and varying speeds are good ways of improving your head control. It is important to be aware of those around you, to know where opponents are. Know where colleagues are. Use the ball when you have controlled it

out of the way, put them to one side, stick your chest out, form a cushion which will absorb the pace of the ball. Use the chest when going forward at the ball. Knock the ball forward, in the air if you want to volley it with left foot or right. It is nearly possible to go through a full circle using just the chest. A ball coming from the front can be played to almost any angle. We can even control the ball by letting it hit the chest, pushing it in the air, ducking under it and turning to go in the opposite direction.

Control with the head will, at this stage, be difficult for you to grasp. But it can be very effective. We control the ball by bending the knees, forming a type of spring. As the ball strikes the head, we collapse the knees, taking weight off the ball and allowing it to drop within controllable distance. We can take the ball in any direction.

Balls that come at us from the front are controlled by taking the head away, leaning back from the ball. Watch the ball very carefully, keeping the eyes open all the time. This is a controlled header.

When practising control with the head or chest, serve or kick the ball into the air so that it can be taken before it bounces.

It is important to make an early selection. Look around and make up your mind quickly. Head tennis is good practice. But the ball must be in the air before we can produce suitable practices.

8 Learning to dribble

This must be allied to *close control*. Close control is having the ball at your feet, where it can be reached quickly. It's running with the ball, but not letting the ball get too far away. If we are put under pressure, we can get to the ball first. Dribbling is actually moving the ball under control. When we go up to a player, with the ball, we try to throw him off balance and beat him by dribbling, as John Barnes, the Liverpool and England winger, does so effectively. We will talk more about these things later.

For close control we use the outside and the inside of the foot. In other words, running with the ball, controlling it with the good foot, inside and outside, taking it where we wish to go. Dribbling involves other parts of the foot, the sole, the heel, the toe, parts of the foot that allow us to change direction quickly.

Along with dribbling and close control we have to add *awareness*. It's no good looking down at the ball all the time, not knowing what is going on around us. We must know where people are, and where others are coming from. We must look up all the time.

Someone is trying to take the ball away from us. Imagine having the ball under the sole of your right foot, putting your body between the ball and an opponent. This is what we call screening. This puts us in a position where we prevent the opponent getting to the ball. But remember to keep moving the ball, otherwise it becomes obstruction.

When taking a ball up to a player, control it with the inside or outside of the foot so

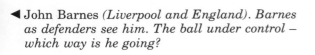
◀ John Barnes *(Liverpool and England). Barnes as defenders see him. The ball under control – which way is he going?*

This is what I call awareness. Without it teamwork breaks down and players become isolated individuals who will eventually be tackled and robbed of the ball

Dribbling needs close control. In other words, having the ball at your feet within a distance which allows you to get it before any challenger and where you can move it and change its direction as you run. This is done with the inside and outside of the foot. But you must not run blindly with your head down. You must see where you are going and know why, so if danger threatens you can put your foot on the ball and stop. You can turn quickly or pass the ball to a team-mate and run for a return pass

Screening the ball is just as important as dribbling. Put your foot on that ball if you cannot run on. Turn quickly and get your body between the ball and any challenging opponent. But remember to keep moving the ball. If you just stand there blocking him it becomes a foul

Beating your opponent in a dribble involves good
balance, good control and total awareness of
exactly where he is and what foot he is on. The
pictures show the simple change of direction.
The inside of the right foot drags the ball towards
the left and your body threatens to accelerate
past the defender's right side. But as he moves
with the forward the defender is losing his edge,
as is proved when the forward puts his foot on
the ball, then lifts his foot over and brings it
down on the inside, pushing the ball back to the
right. This wrong-foots the defender long
enough for the forward to make ground

that you can change direction quickly,
throwing him off balance. Imagine taking a
ball to a player using the inside of the foot,
threatening to accelerate away to the left.
Maybe he will start to come with us. Then
by stopping the ball and using the outside of
the foot, changing direction quickly, we
would probably throw him off balance long
enough to get by him on his left.

If the ball can be nicked away by a defender, use the foot to drag it back as he moves in to tackle, then turn away and go. The word accelerate is important because when your dribble technique has lost the defender for a few precious seconds, you must make use of those seconds by getting away from him, either to run on or to make an accurate pass

Movement of the body while on the ball leaves defenders unsure of your intentions. If you simply stand with the ball and look around, you are providing opponents with a solid target. But if you move, even slightly, shifting your balance over the ball, nobody is sure which way you intend going. This gives you an element of surprise

Here we see three players, each controlling a ball, attempting to keep their ball in a confined dribbling space as well as trying to nick away one of the balls controlled by their team-mates. This is good for control and for building competitive spirit

Georgie Best was probably one of the best 'attacking dribblers'. He went at people with the ball, showing it to them, but always out of reach. Then, when they went for it, he pulled the ball away and accelerated.

Dribbling tends to be done slowly. Add *acceleration* so that when we have thrown the opponent off balance, we can get away quickly.

We use the sole of the foot when dribbling close. We can drag the ball away with the sole of our foot, remembering all the time that we should be looking around for someone to pass to, or waiting for an opportunity to accelerate away. **Good balance**, **close control**, **aggressive acceleration** – all these are important factors.

The use of the body to throw players off balance is vital. Swing the body to the left and right while controlling the ball. This will help to confuse the opponent.

Practices

When learning to dribble, we must develop a 'feel' for the ball. This can be done in various ways. I like to give each player a ball in an area the size of the six-yard box. Use as many players as you like, and ask them to dribble the ball, using the sole of the foot, the outside, the inside, but trying to avoid each other. Make a little game of it: keep your own ball, but at the same time try to knock someone else's ball out of the square. One player should finish up with his ball.

Dribbling can be overdone. Remember that dribbling is a way of beating an opponent, of holding the ball and screening it until one of our own players supports. It

Three players have possession with one player challenging. This encourages intelligent dribbling as well as creating an awareness of who is close at hand to take a pass and who is making good angles. It also stops needless dribbling

may be the prelude to a pass or the chance to look around. Add close control and it's a way of running with the ball while taking charge of a situation.

Small-sided games in small squares, ten by ten yards or thereabouts, are good for dribbling and close control practices. Players are put under gentle pressure. If players hold the ball for a few seconds, this will encourage dribbling, and at the same time make them aware that someone is trying to take it away from them. It also emphasizes the fact that you only control and dribble the ball until you get support.

To control dribbling, use the same sort of square. Insist that the pass made by the player controlling the ball is made to the player furthest away. This allows him time to control it. Then insist that he tries to beat a player before making a pass. The challenge shouldn't be too severe, and the area should be large enough to allow the players time and room.

The player learns to screen, learns to dribble and learns to pass within the dribbling and control techniques. A time limit of four or five seconds when holding the ball is long enough, and will give all the players an opportunity to practise every twenty or thirty seconds.

Close control, dribbling and *aggressive running*. This is increasing the pace of the dribbling and running with the ball. Having controlled the ball, having sold a dummy, accelerate. The dummies, the changes of balance and the feints still apply when the running becomes more aggressive.

We add aggression because we are moving much faster. We don't run flat out but

Now the man on the ball must find and pass to the player furthest away from him. This gives the player taking the pass more time to control the ball and opens up the game, preventing congestion in corners of the pitch. Now the man in possession must go at an opponent with the ball and beat him, before he can make a pass

usually run at three-quarters speed, leaving room for acceleration when challenged.

This is positive movement, running and throwing the dummy, playing the ball past, and accelerating. We can slow down and accelerate, we can change direction, we can stop and accelerate in a different direction. When we attack a defender at speed, he will attempt to match our speed. This is where we need aggression and purpose to get the ball past him on the other side. It is important not to let the ball get too far away, or too close to the opponent. The ball should be far enough in front to tempt him, but close enough to ensure that if he makes his tackle, we can knock the ball past him.

My brother, Bobby Charlton, was probably the best runner with the ball we have seen in English football. More recently there has been no one to match Diego Maradona, the amazingly gifted Argentinian who turns out for Napoli. Maradona is so powerful that whenever he bears down on goal, defenders are inclined to panic as England did in the

Diego Maradona *(Napoli and Argentina). The world's greatest player destroys England in the 1986 World Cup*

Here the player on the ball
swerves past his opponent,
using good body movements,
picks his spot and shoots across
the goalkeeper as he moves off
his line. Regulate the practice
so that players don't spend
more than four or five seconds
on the ball. This will speed
things up

This time the attacker shows the defender just enough of the ball to tempt him, then knocks the ball past him and accelerates after it. The defender is at an immediate disadvantage because he must turn and follow, but the forward is into his stride and going the way he is facing

Aggression, confidence and determination are all shown on this lad's face as he takes the ball up to a defender, dummies him, then moves smoothly past him to take up a goal-scoring position. This is a good little three-man game, one forward, one defender and a goalkeeper. The defender must do all within his power to prevent the forward getting in his shot. The forward must beat the defender before he can shoot. All three players sharpen their play

1986 World Cup in Mexico. Move fast enough to tempt players when you are favourite. Add aggression and determination to running with the ball, otherwise you could be forced off it when you should be in charge.

Practices

Have a target at the end of aggressive running. Practise with goals and a goal-keeper, one against one, and insist that a player has to take another on in order to get a shot in while under some sort of pressure. Now this can be done at any age; you don't need to be fully grown to apply this type of training. It can be done with very small kids. It also gives them good shooting practice.

We can add two against one situations, again with a target. You get great success with this. Two players run very quickly at an opponent, threaten to take him on, but

We go back to that typical situation where the player going wide finds himself heading up a dead-end. So good team-play comes into it. He checks back, pulls the ball away from the defender and lays it off to a team-mate who shoots for goal. All the ingredients are there – good dribbling, awareness of those around him, an accurate pass, steady control by the man taking the pass and a low hard shot, well taken by the goalkeeper. These three-man games are excellent for working on all the varied situations which players face

stop. This makes the opponent stop, but not quickly enough. Change direction or make a pass to the other player. The defender must run to him also, and as the defender comes from a different angle the player with possession should knock the ball past him.

Always go at a player. Occasionally, we need to dribble, because we have stopped and the pass isn't on. Then we must hold the ball until we get support. Two against one situations with a target provide more realistic practices.

Conditioned Games

Condition games so that the player receiving the ball must hold it for a few seconds.

Let players make mistakes, let them put other players under pressure by running at them with the ball at every opportunity. By doing this they will learn timing and control, and how to be effective. Do condition the games. Don't play four-a-side and leave it at that. In everything we do – passing, dribbling, ball control – conditioned games will help.

When learning chest and head control it is important to get the ball off the ground which is better done in conditioned games.

Encourage players to dribble, to attack with the ball. Encourage aggressive running. Condition the games. The aim is to improve technique in realistic situations, but remember, *not too quickly*. Don't make things too difficult.